TRADITION AND INNOVATION
IN THE POETRY OF
DAFYDD AP GWILYM

by

Rachel Bromwich

CARDIFF
UNIVERSITY OF WALES PRESS

1972

First Edition , 1967

Reprinted , 1972

© University of Wales Press, 1972

0 7083 0168 1

PREFACE

This essay is based upon a lecture delivered before the Honourable Society of Cymmrodorion in London on 29 November 1963. In an earlier form it was the subject of an O'Donnell lecture delivered in the University of Wales in March 1962. I wish to express my thanks to the Council of the Honourable Society of Cymmrodorion for giving their permission to re-issue the essay, which was first published in the *Transactions* of the Society for the year 1964. I am indebted to the Editor of the *Transactions*, Professor Idris Foster, for some valuable comments and criticisms upon my original draft. This new edition has been prepared at the invitation of the University of Wales Press Board, and it incorporates a few minor alterations and additions to the text. I have endeavoured also to bring the bibliographical references up to date.

Rachel Bromwich

January 1967

TRADITION AND INNOVATION IN THE POETRY OF DAFYDD AP GWILYM

THE Honourable Society of Cymmrodorion has had a long and close association with the study of Dafydd ap Gwilym. This association may indeed be said to have started as far back as the year 1789, when Owain Myfyr (a former secretary of the Society) financed and organized the publication of the first edition of Dafydd ap Gwilym's poems—an enterprise in which he was ably assisted by another London Welshman, William Owen Pughe.[1] What we may call the international aspects of Dafydd ap Gwilym's poetry have claimed the attention of scholars for nearly a century,[2] and important pioneer articles on this subject appeared in *Y Cymmrodor* for the year 1878 by Professor E. B. Cowell, and in the Society's *Transactions* for the years 1906-8 by the Rev. G. Hartwell Jones, the Rev. J. Machreth Rees and Professor W. Lewis Jones.[3]

---

[1] Owen Jones and William Owen Pughe: *Barddoniaeth Dafydd ap Gwilym* (London, 1789). This work was based primarily on the manuscript collections made by the Morris brothers, and the publication was officially sponsored by the Gwyneddigion. See T. Parry, 'Barddoniaeth Dafydd ap Gwilym, 1789', *Journal of the Welsh Bibliographical Society*, VIII (1954-7), pp. 189 ff.; *Gwaith Dafydd ap Gwilym*, pp. lxxvi, clxv-ix; *History of the Cymmrodorion*, p. 97.

[2] It would have been more exact to say 'nearly two centuries', had Iolo Morganwg chosen to publish his conclusions on this matter. Professor G. J. Williams has noted that Iolo's unpublished papers contain evidence that he, nearly a century before all subsequent scholars, had observed a resemblance between certain of the themes of Dafydd ap Gwilym and those of the Troubadours. See G. J. Williams, 'Iolo Morganwg', *Annual Lecture of the BBC in Wales* (1963), pp. 7-8.

[3] E. B. Cowell, 'Dafydd ab Gwilym', *Y Cymmrodor*, II (1878), pp. 101 ff.; G. Hartwell Jones, 'Italian Influence on Celtic Literature', *Trans.*, 1905-6, pp. 84 ff.; J. Machreth Rees, 'Dafydd ap Gwilym a'i Gyfnod', *ibid.*, pp. 31 ff.; W. Lewis Jones, 'The Literary Relationships of Dafydd ap Gwilym', *Trans.*, 1907-8, pp. 118 ff.

All these essays were directed towards setting Dafydd's poetry in a European context: they examined external parallels and suggested the possibility of foreign literary influences. Then, in the *Transactions* for 1913-14, Sir Ifor Williams's long discussion[1] inaugurated a new era in the study of this aspect of the poet's work.

All these, and certain other early studies,[2] came to be synthesized and developed further in a monumental book by a Dutch scholar, the late Theodor Chotzen, whose *Recherches sur la Poésie de Dafydd ap Gwilym* was published at Amsterdam in 1927. This has remained until the present day the standard work on the subject of Dafydd's indebtedness to foreign literature and ideas—a mine of information for all investigators. Nevertheless, it would be difficult to name any one of the contributory studies drawn upon by Chotzen which has not seen very great advances in the forty years which have now elapsed since the publication of his book. First and foremost, we now have an inestimable advantage in Dr. Thomas Parry's critical edition, *Gwaith Dafydd ap Gwilym* (1952)—a major work of scholarship which has made substantial progress towards determining the linguistic and metrical criteria by which we may distinguish the *cywyddau* of the fourteenth century from those which are of later date. We now have a working basis which Chotzen did not have, and it is inevitable that it should make necessary the modification of some of his conclusions.

In one sense, of course, it is true that the output of a major poet can stand above the quest for sources. This view is indeed frequently taken by the literary critic, who would claim that the investigation of sources can have no relevant bearing on our appreciation of a poet's work, and is of interest purely as a matter of literary history. I do not

---

[1]'Dafydd ap Gwilym a'r Glêr', *Trans.*, 1913-14, pp. 83-204.

[2]The most important of these was L. C. Stern, 'Davydd ab Gwilym, ein walisischer Minnesänger', *Zeitschrift für celtische Philologie*, VII, pp. 1-251.

believe, however, that questions of literary sources and influences can ultimately be separated from questions of literary value: all such studies may contribute to the appreciation of a poet's response to his intellectual surroundings, and so to the comprehension of his achievement.[1] The investigation of such literary influences as may have reached Dafydd from outside Wales, and the manner in which he responded to them, is one which I do not think can properly be neglected from any full study of his versatile genius: it is also one to which scholarship in recent years has paid the least attention, and which certainly needs re-examination now that we have the new edition. In the case of Dafydd ap Gwilym, I suggest also that such studies may even have their part to play in determining what individual qualities of style and treatment can be recognized as distinguishing his authentic work from that of his contemporaries and successors. And this is, after all, the major problem which confronts the present generation with respect to Dafydd ap Gwilym: for, in a manner comparable to his remote predecessors Aneirin and Taliesin, the distinction recognized both by his contemporaries and by succeeding generations has caused the accumulation round his name of a mass of spurious verse. Thus Dr. Parry's intensive study of fourteenth-century language and metrics has reduced the

[1]'Considered in its full implication, the problem of literary influence is an integral part of the problem of literary creation, and this can never be differentiated—not to say solved—until what a writer of genius does with his material becomes the object of a more intuitive type of scholarship than is common today.'—P. Mansell-Jones, *Background of Modern French Poetry* (Cambridge, 1951) p. vii. These words have been quoted by Professor E. Vinaver as a preliminary to his study of the use made by Sir Thomas Malory of his antecedent French sources, *The Arthurian Legend in the Middle Ages*, ed. R. S. Loomis (Oxford, 1959), p. 546. They are no less appropriate to the study of Dafydd ap Gwilym's poetry, even though the external influences upon his work are far less easily traced than is the case with Malory.

canon of the poems which he regards as authentic to rather over half the number which are attributed to Dafydd in the 1789 edition, and less than half of those which are attributed to him in the manuscripts. Even if it should turn out that this estimate requires further extension or modification in the future, it can safely be presumed that much dead wood has now been cleared away, and, as a result, it is already apparent that contemporary scholarship is beginning to turn to the problem of what may constitute personal characteristics in the poet's work, in a way which was hardly possible before.

In the last forty years, also, much fresh work has been done upon the literary works in other languages which have most bearing on the study of Dafydd ap Gwilym: on Troubadour poetry, on the medieval lyric in Latin, French and English, and on the influence of Ovid on the Middle Ages—particularly in respect to a very relevant and influential French poem of the thirteenth century, that is, the *Roman de la Rose*.[1] Again, on the purely Welsh side, much progress has taken place in the last forty years in the study of the poets who were Dafydd's predecessors, contemporaries and immediate successors, upon the early bardic grammars,[2] upon the development of *cynghanedd* and of the *cywydd* metre—and here again I must refer to the important contributions published in the *Transactions* of

---

[1] A few outstanding titles must suffice: F. J. E. Raby, *Secular Latin Poetry in the Middle Ages* (1934: second ed. 1957); A. Jeanroy, *La Poésie Lyrique des Troubadours* (1934); C. S. Lewis, *The Allegory of Love* (1936); G. Paré, *Les ideés et les lettres au XIIIe siècle: Le Roman de la Rose,* (Montreal, 1947); Carleton Brown, *English Lyrics of the Thirteenth Century* (1932); G. L. Brook, *The Harley Lyrics* (1948). The Welsh affinities of the Harley Lyrics have become even clearer in the years which have elapsed since Sir Ifor Williams first drew attention to their importance in relation to Dafydd's literary background. To this list should now be added P. Dronke, *Medieval Latin and the Rise of European Love Lyric* (Oxford, 1965).

[2] G. J. Williams and E. J. Jones, *Gramadegau'r Penceirddiaid* (Cardiff, 1934).

this Society in the 1930's by Professor W. J. Gruffydd[1] and by Dr. Thomas Parry,[2] and to the volume devoted to Sir Idris Bell's study of the poet in 1942.[3] Progress has also been made in the editing and evaluation of the *canu rhydd*,[4] and this too has its importance in relation to Dafydd ap Gwilym. All branches of these studies have seen such rapid progress in the last years, and are continuing to progress in such a way that my remarks now can only be regarded as of an interim nature. I should like, then, to try to re-define a few of the many outstanding problems concerning Dafydd ap Gwilym—problems which, in any case, it is easier to set forth than to provide with satisfactory answers. And, incidentally, I should like to stress the importance for this study of work which has been proceeding in other fields and has, for the most part, been quite differently orientated. For instance, much of the research that has gone into the social and literary background of Chaucer's poetry has its relevance for the study of his near-contemporary Dafydd ap Gwilym. [5]Then, if we look at the literature of the country which is Wales's other neighbour, across the sea, we find that in Ireland during the life-time of Dafydd ap Gwilym, the third Earl of Desmond was engaged in composing love-poetry on the French model, but in the strict metres of Irish bardic verse—a parallel fusing of the Celtic with the continental tradition to that which was taking place in Wales at the

[1]'Rhagarweiniad i Farddoniaeth Cymru cyn Dafydd ap Gwilym', *Trans.*, 1937, pp. 257 ff.

[2]'Twf y Gynghanedd', *Trans.*, 1936, pp. 143 ff.; 'Datblygiad y Cywydd', *Trans.*, 1939, pp. 209 ff.

[3]*Dafydd ap Gwilym: Fifty Poems*; with Introductory Essays by Idris Bell and David Bell (Hon. Soc. Cymmrodorion, 1942).

[4]T. H. Parry-Williams, *Canu Rhydd Cynnar* (Cardiff, 1932); Brinley Rees, *Dulliau'r Canu Rhydd* (Cardiff, 1952); D. Gwenallt Jones, *Y Ficer Prichard* a '*Canwyll y Cymry*' (n.d.).

[5]Our understanding of the social background of Welsh poetry in the fourteenth century has been enriched by the publication of Glanmor Williams' *The Welsh Church from Conquest to Reformation* (Cardiff, 1962).

same time.[1]   In Ireland also, the thesis has been recently
advanced that many of the themes of medieval French
courtly verse were introduced in the wake of the Norman
Conquest, to survive by a long sub-literary tradition
which eventually came to the surface in the popular free-
metre poetry of the seventeenth and eighteenth centuries.[2]
There is here the possibility of an analogy which could have
considerable importance for the relation subsisting between Dafydd's poetry and certain of the themes in the
Welsh *canu rhydd*, a subject about which we know all too
little as yet.

I have taken 'Tradition and Innovation' as my title,
because in order to form any estimate of the new influences
which came into Welsh poetry with Dafydd ap Gwilym
and his contemporaries, it is of course necessary to
examine both sides of the question, and to try to under-
stand as much as we can about the literary inheritance
which Dafydd received from his predecessors. Here I
should like to quote the words in which, after the lapse of
a quarter of a century, Sir Ifor Williams alluded retro-
spectively to the conviction which inspired his own study
of this subject[3]:

'(Ni) fedrwn i ddeall canu Dafydd ap Gwilym heb fynd y tu allan
i Gymru. Fedrwn i mo'i ddeall ef chwaith heb gofio ei ddyled i
feirdd ei wlad ei hun yn y canrifoedd o'i flaen ef. Mewn llenyddiaeth
fyw ceir dwy duedd sy'n mantoli ei gilydd, sef cadw'r hen, a chro-
esawu'r newydd. Bob tro y cawn fudiad llenyddol newydd ym

---

[1]On Gerald third Earl of Desmond (1359-98), see T. F. O'Rahilly,
Dánta Grádha (Cork, 1926), no. 4, and introduction by R. Flower;
R. Flower, *The Irish Tradition* (Oxford, 1947), pp. 143-4 (here 'fourth'
should read 'third earl'; see G. Murphy, *Eigse II*, p. 64.). The
duanaire or poem-book of Gerald the Earl from the fifteenth-century
Book of Fermoy has recently been edited (in Irish) for the first time by
Gearóid mac Niocaill, *Studia Hibernica*, 3 (1963), pp. 7 ff. Cf. J. E.
Caerwyn Williams, *Traddodiad Llenyddol Iwerddon*, pp. 153-4; Frank
O'Connor, *Kings, Lords, and Commons* (London, 1961), p. x.

[2]Seán Ó Tuama, *An Grá in Amhráin na nDaoine* (Dublin, 1960).

[3]*Trans.* 1938, pp. 52-3.

mywyd Cymru, dyna sy'n digwydd ieuo'n gymharus elfennau
Cymreig ag elfennau estron, a ffrwyth y briodas honno fydd
genedigaeth a chreadigaeth newydd, arbennig i'n gwlad a'n cenedl
ni.'

Dr. Parry's edition begins with a series of twenty-one
bardic poems, composed partly, but not wholly, in the
older metres of the *englyn* and *awdl*, and in the conventional
style: some of them, at least, are to be attributed to the
poet's early career. They deal with the traditional themes
of twelfth- and thirteenth-century bardic poetry: eulogy
and elegy addressed to patrons, an interesting example of
satire, and a handful of religious poems.[1] This group
includes the important praise-poems to Dafydd's patron,
Ifor Hael, whose authenticity Dr. Parry has indeed
questioned, but on external rather than on internal
evidence, and this evidence has subsequently received a
different interpretation by other scholars.[2] These bardic
poems as a group express all the old *ethos* of the Gogynfeirdd: the praise of noble descent and the virtues of
courage and generosity, with the repeated assertion that
the bard's patron has no peer,[3] the interdependence of
bard and patron, and the idea of the intimate relation
subsisting between a ruler and his territory, which
commemorates his death by storms and swollen rivers.
The *marwnadau* re-iterate the persistent Celtic elegiac
theme of the lament for the deserted home, and the
manner in which the poet addresses the dead man directly,

---

[1] To those included in GDG should now be added the *englynion*
'I'r Grog o Gaer', *Llawysgrif Hendregadredd*, pp. 312-3; see *Gwaith
Dafydd ap Gwilym (Ail Argraffiad*, 1963), pp. xix, 556.

[2] Saunders Lewis, *Llên Cymru*, II, pp. 201-2; Dafydd Bowen,
'Dafydd ap Gwilym a Morgannwg', *Llên Cymru* V, pp. 164-73. For a
discussion of the evidence, and a further suggestion, see now GDG[2],
pp. xix-xxii, and a note by Gwyn Thomas, *Llên Cymru*, VII, pp.
249-251.

[3] The figure corresponds with Curtius's *topoi* of 'inexpressibility' and
'outdoing'; *European Literature and the Latin Middle Ages* (English edn.
1962), pp. 159, 162.

calling on him to rise up and answer, is another feature typical of laments both in Welsh and in Irish. The imagery characteristic of the praise-poetry of preceding centuries is recurrent: Llywelyn and Ifor are, in turn, referred to metaphorically as a stag, a hawk, a lion, an eagle. The full range of reference to the characters of early heroic tradition is employed for the purpose of eulogy: Ifor Hael derives the epithet which has clung to him from a comparison of his generosity with that of Nudd, Rhydderch and Mordaf, the ancient triad of the *Tri Hael*[1] or Three Generous Men (GDG. 7, 10), and Dafydd compares Ifor's home to *neuadd Reged*—the hall of Taliesin's patron, Urien—and speaks of himself as another Taliesin, for the rewards which he has received from Ifor (GDG. 9, 33-35; 10, 27-34). Again, the *marwnad* to Llywelyn describes him as *Deifr helgud* (GDG. 13, 13), 'pursuer of the men of Deira'—by now an epithet which must have lost much of its meaning,[2] but one which leads directly back to the cradle of Welsh poetic tradition in the old British North, and implies a familiarity on the part of Dafydd's audience with all the old concepts of praise-poetry. The antithesis of all this encomiastic imagery was traditionally expressed by the Court Poets in satire and abuse—and we have as an example Dafydd's satire on a rival poet, Rhys Meigen (GDG. 21), whose personal characteristics and wretched verse are attacked in a string of englynion so involved and obscure in their range of abuse that it is almost possible to credit the later story to the effect that the unfortunate victim fell down dead as the result of hearing them. Whether true or false, the tradition is a forcible reminder of the supernatural power

[1]On the outstanding popularity of this triad among the bards at all periods, see my *Trioedd Ynys Prydein*, pp. 5-6, and introduction pp. lxxv-vi.

[2]Cf. Dr. Parry's note, GDG, pp. 448-9. This conclusion gains emphasis when we recall Llywelyn's circumstances; he had sworn allegiance to the Black Prince in 1343 (GDG, p. xxvii).

which was always attributed to the words of the poet in
early Celtic society; and there are many comparable
examples in Irish of the devastating effects brought about
by a poet's satire, as well as of the extortionate demands
the poets were enabled to make by reason of the fear of
being satirized. As late as the fifteenth century, a parallel
instance is recorded of an Irish poet's satire causing death.[1]
Satire and eulogy were in both countries the two com-
plementary facets of the bardic tradition, and the deadly
effects attributed to the one emphasize by implication the
great social significance attached to the other. All
professional poets must indeed be able to show their paces
in both, as is recognized by Dafydd in his contention with
Gruffudd Gryg, when he offers his opponent a contest in
words, as an alternative to one with swords, and Gruffudd
then refers back to the earlier incident by asserting that he
is not a Rhys Meigen to be slain by satire (GDG. 150,
39-44; 151, 70). In all these bardic poems, Dafydd shows
himself to be an adept in the earlier metrical techniques,
and with all the resources of the traditional learning at his
command. This is apparent in the richness of his vocabulary, imagery, and allusion to historical and legendary
matter, including the knowledge he shows of old legal
terminology. We can observe the apparatus of praise-
poetry being transferred into the new *cywydd* metre, and
these poems give evidence that Dafydd could excel in the
cywydd mawl no less than in the *cywydd serch*. But I think it
is noticeable that the older modes of expression are used
for what is most deeply felt, and thus it is the *englyn* or a
combination of *englyn* and *toddaid* which are used in the
personal laments composed on the death of his uncle, of

---

[1]Sir John Stanley, Lord Lieutenant of Ireland, was satirized by
Niall Ó'hUiginn, and 'lived after this satire but five weeks, for he died
of the virulence of the lampoons'. The event is said to have taken
place in 1414 (*Annals of the Four Masters*, ed. John O'Donovan (Dublin,
1848), II, p. 819). See also J. E. Caerwyn Williams, *op. cit.*, p. 147.

Ifor Hael and of Angharad,[1] while the *cywydd* is employed
for the more formal lament for Rhydderch (composed on
behalf of another person) and for the fictitious *marwnadau*
to fellow-poets still living.

Dr. Parry has shown that the adaptation of the *cywydd* to
praise-poetry was a metrical innovation of the fourteenth
century, for which Dafydd can no longer be held as
personally responsible.[2] In a great number of ways, the
themes and techniques of the older poetry were carried
over into the new metre; and it is, in the first place, as an
example of this continuity of the accepted moulds of
bardic expression that I would like to refer to Dafydd's
Ymryson with Gruffudd Gryg. For contentions in verse
between rival poets were a feature of the common Celtic
bardic tradition, and go back to an early date both in
Wales and in Ireland. Although there was a general and
widespread fondness throughout the Middle Ages for
debates of all kinds, the form given to this contest can be
fully accounted for as arising out of native poetic conventions, whatever may be said as to the deeper issues
which are involved in it. I think, therefore, that there is
no need to attach much weight to the comparison which
has been made at various times between the form of the
Ymryson and the poetic debates which occur in Provençal
poetry[3] as a framework for discussing a wide range of

[1]GDG, 16. Considering its authorship, this poem is striking in its
conformity with the older tradition; as an elegy on a woman, it
invites comparison with Gruffudd ap Maredudd's *awdl* to Gwen-
hwyfar o Fôn, *Oxford Book of Welsh Verse*, no. 38, rather than with any
of Dafydd ap Gwilym's other work.

[2]*Trans.*, 1939, p. 215.

[3]The types known as the *tenso* and the *joc parti* have been somewhat tentatively compared with the form of the *Ymryson*, though any
connexion between the two was rejected by Ifor Williams, *Trans.*,
1913-14, p. 121. For references to the opinions expressed on this
matter, see Chotzen, *op. cit.*, p. 17. The greater antiquity of the Welsh
contests is pointed out by T. Gwynn Jones, 'Bardism and Romance',
Trans., 1913-14, p. 296; but he does not cite the supporting evidence
for their antiquity which comes from Ireland.

abstract problems—for the Celtic precedents are much older than these. Their existence, indeed, is indicated among the earliest poetic traditions in both countries,[1] and the form continued to be used long after the Middle Ages. Thus it is interesting to find that the opposition between north and south Wales, which is played upon by Dafydd ap Gwilym and Gruffudd Gryg, is paralleled on a far larger scale in Irish as late as the seventeenth century, in a long bardic contention between poets representing the north and south of Ireland:[2] one suspects that there could have been earlier precedents which have not come down for this aspect of the controversy, since in both countries certain recognized literary tendencies have always distinguished the north from the south. In Wales, the *Ymryson* between Dafydd and Gruffudd Gryg may be regarded as a reflection of the recurrent opposition between the conservative tenacity of the north, and the south's more ready receptivity to new literary modes.[3] The earliest contests in both languages represent a kind of

---

[1] The evidence for *stories* about bardic contests goes back in both countries to the ninth or tenth century, and is of such a kind as to imply that the custom itself is far older. In Wales, it consists of the traditions about Taliesin's contest with the bards of Maelgwn Gwynedd (on the date of which see Ifor Williams, *Chwedl Taliesin,* 1957), and of Nennius's account of the contest between Ambrosius and the *magi* of Vortigern. With these, cf. the Irish tale *Immacallam in dá Thuarad,* the 'Colloquy of the Two Sages' (ed. Whitley Stokes, *Revue Celtique,* XXVI, pp. 4-64). A ninth-century date is proposed by K. Jackson, *Man,* XXXIV (May, 1934), p. 67. Further evidence as to the existence of such contests may be adduced from the Welsh Laws and manuscripts of the early poetry.

[2] *Iomarbháigh na bhFileadh.* 'The Contention of the Poets', ed. and trans. Lambert McKenna, *Irish Texts Society,* vols. XX, XXI. See E. Knott, *Irish Classical Poetry,* pp. 74 ff.; Caerwyn Williams, *op. cit.,* p. 173.

[3] W. J. Gruffydd, *Llenyddiaeth Cymru,* 1450-1600, pp. 67-8: 'Y Gogledd sy'n cadw, y Dê sy'n cychwyn.' For Ireland cf. Alwyn and Brinley Rees, *Celtic Heritage* (London, 1961), p. 101.

jockeying for position between rival poets, sometimes with
a definite appointment as *pencerdd* to a certain patron as
their reward, as in the contest for supremacy between
Cynddelw Brydydd Mawr and Seisyll Bryffwrch at the
court of Madog ap Maredudd,[1] and probably in Phylip
Brydydd's contest with the *gofeirdd* or inferior poets at the
court of Rhys Ieuanc.[2]   But in Dafydd's contest with
Gruffudd Gryg, as again in the most interesting of the later
Welsh contests of which we have record,[3] the matter at
issue is some fundamental difference between the partici-
pants as to the theory and practice of poetry—one might
say, therefore, that these bardic controversies represent the
earliest examples of literary criticism in Welsh. They tend
also to take the form of a debate between a poetic in-
novator on the one hand, and the 'Establishment' upon
the other.   But Gruffudd Gryg, who came from the
commote of Llifon in Anglesey,[4] and was somewhat
junior to Dafydd ap Gwilym, is a poet whose own surviving
compositions hardly qualify him as a satisfactory exponent
of the conservative bardic standpoint, since they are all
cywyddau, and *cywyddau* which show at times a *finesse* and
versatility in theme and treatment which rival Dafydd's
own.[5]   It may be said of some of these poems, however,
that the weightier character of the subject-matter dealt
with throws a possible light on Gruffudd's criticism of
Dafydd; moreover, they include no *fabliaux* or poems of

[1]*Llawysgrif Hendregadredd*, pp. 180-181.

[2]*ibid.*, pp. 226-229. See T. Gwynn Jones, 'Bardism and Romance'.
Trans., 1913-14, pp. 240-1, 290-294.

[3]i.e. those of Rhys Goch Eryri with Siôn Cent and Llywelyn ap y
Moel on the nature of poetic inspiration, and the seventeenth-century
contest between Edmund Prys and William Cynwal.

[4]On the Anglesey connexions and date of Gruffudd Gryg, see
E. D. Jones, *National Library of Wales Journal*, X, pp. 230-1. His poem
I'r Lleuad (*Oxford Book*, no. 56), with its reference to *tir Harri*, proves
that he was alive at the end of the century. See Ifor Williams's note,
DGG , p. 228, and introduction, pp. xcviii-xcix.

[5]Cf. T. Parry, *Trans.*, 1939, pp. 213-4.

love-escapades, and Gruffudd's *cywyddau* to girls are recognizably in the older tradition of the *rhieingerddi* composed by the court poets. It would be interesting to know whether these *cywyddau* are in fact all poems of Gruffudd Gryg's later career, and if they were composed after the *Ymryson* was concluded. I shall return later to the substance of Gruffudd Gryg's attack upon Dafydd's poetry.

These, then, are the poems for whose framework Dafydd ap Gwilym is in one way or another indebted to earlier bardic models. They represent only a small part of his total output, and it is not, of course, on these, but on his far more numerous *cywyddau serch* that his distinctive reputation in succeeding generations has been based. For the greater part of his work, as it has come down to us, comprises those poems of personal situation which introduce a whole range of new themes, barely—if at all— touched upon in Welsh poetry of the previous generations, in so far as the extant evidence can tell us. These are the poems of love and nature, centred on the attendant circumstances of the woodland *oed*, the meeting-place to which he invites Morfudd or Dyddgu or some un-named girl: tales of broken appointments and frustrations of various kinds, such as losing his way in the dark or the mist, the interference of 'Yr Eiddig' or the competition of other lovers, and the poems more specifically concerned with love-escapades, such as *Trafferth mewn Tafarn* (GDG. 124), and *Y Cwt Gwyddau* (GDG. 126). The last has the three stock figures of the Wife, the Jealous Husband and the Clerk-lover (that is, Dafydd himself), like the international *fabliaux* to which these poems as a class bear some relation. Then there are the poems in which Dafydd champions the advantages of the natural life against the austerity advocated to him by the friars. In all these poems, the detailed and sensitive nature descriptions which we associate particularly with Dafydd ap Gwilym are, for the most part, very loosely and indirectly linked with the main theme, and this is particularly apparent in

the group of *llatai*[1] or love-messenger poems, where the
poet's chief interest is in elaborating the *dyfalu* or de-
scriptive address to a bird or an animal.

Yet even here, where we might least expect to find them,
in the poems whose subject-matter has almost no real
precedent in earlier Welsh poetry, many facets of the older
tradition of praise-poetry can be traced. There are the
stock comparisons for a girl's beauty, taken over from the
Gogynfeirdd.[2]   Among the most popular of these in the
older poetry were comparisons with the beauty of moving
water, both of sea-foam and the rough water of rivers—in
such recurrent phrases as *deuliw y don* and *hoen geirw
afonydd*; with all forms of light, especially of the dawn—
gorne gwawr fore—and of the sun, moon and stars, candles
and lamps;[3] with gossamer—*gwawn wedd*; and the very
popular comparisons with snow—*gorlliw eiry mân* (GDG.
42, 2), *hoen eiry di-frisg* (GDG. 33, 18), and the like. All
these and others,[4] recur constantly with minor verbal

---

[1]The question of the literary antecedents of this type of poem is
complicated, and their style suggests a connexion with the *cywyddau
gofyn*. Another view has linked the *llatai* poems with the *gorhoffedd*
poems of the Gogynfeirdd, some of which contain an address to the
poet's horse; see T. Gwynn Jones, *Rhieingerddi'r Gogynfeirdd*, pp. 17-26,
41-2; T. Parry, *Hanes Llenyddiaeth Gymraeg*, p. 87; Saunders Lewis,
Braslun o Hanes Llenyddiaeth Gymraeg, pp. 90-91.

[2]For the earlier instances see T. Gwynn Jones, *Rhieingerddi*, pp.
27-31; for some additional examples from Dafydd ap Gwilym and his
contemporaries, see Chotzen, *op. cit.*, pp. 204 ff.

[3]Exx: *cannwyll Gwynedd* (GDG, 111 22); *Fy nghariad oleuad lamp*
(GDG 37, 2); *bryd wyth wiwlamp* (GDG 35, 54); *llugorn llon* (GDG
81, 28).

[4]Chotzen (*op. cit.*, p. 203) makes the important point that some of
the more unusual of these stock comparisons appear also in Irish
poetry, but that they appear to be restricted to Irish and Welsh.
These include the comparisons with gossamer (*loyne gwawn*, GDG 54,
26; *gwawn ei gwedd*, GDG 85, 48); with lime (*dyn galch*, GDG 42, 19);
and of the hair and eyebrows with the colour of the blackbird (*ail blu
mwyalch*, GDG 30, 39; *Duach yw'r gwallt / no mwyalch*, GDG 45, 30-1).

Continued on next page

changes[1] in Dafydd's poetry, though the manner in which he uses them may be sometimes lightly ironical,[2] so that the reader is led to expect that more subtle nuances of implication may at any time be present than when these same phrases are used by Dafydd's more conservative contemporaries, Iolo Goch and Gruffudd ap Maredudd. He frequently introduces the names of the traditional heroines, *Indeg, Tegau, Luned,* and others. Again, Dafydd pays his tribute of admiration by composing poetry, *gwawd y tafawd,* in honour of the girl he is addressing (84, 2); he tells us that he makes public her praise, singing it in the presence of lords at feasts or else causing others—the *clêr ofer* or lesser poets—to do so (85, 11, 23), and by this means spreading her fame through all Gwynedd (34, 14), throughout Wales (137, 15), or as far as the English border (85, 23).[3] Just as in the conventional praise-poetry, a generous material payment was counted on by the bard from his patron, so Dafydd plainly considered himself as equally entitled to a definite reward for his labours in the form of favours from the girl, and, of course, his frequently reiterated complaint is that he does not receive this reward.[4] Similarly, he can threaten a girl who has cast him off with the powerful weapon of satire (7, 17-20). There are suggestions in the earlier *rhieingerddi*

Continued from previous page

They point both to the antiquity and to the independence of the Celtic *formula* for ideal beauty. The whole subject needs further investigation.

[1]Exx: *unne dydd* (GDG 85, 6); *goleudon lafarfron liw* (42, 5); *Hoen geirw tes* (39, 40); *dyn eiry peilliw* (37, 37); *od gawad* (52, 20).

[2]Obvious examples are *haul Wynedd* (128, 5); *lliw haul dwyrain* (124, 9); but in many instances the irony is more subtle; cf. for instance the series of epithets addressed to Morfudd in the poem *Gofyn Cymod* (GDG 52)—or, in a different way, the epithets applied to the nuns (GDG 113, 17-22).

[3]This seems to be the implication of the phrase *hyd eithaf Ceri*, if *Ceri* here means the commote in Montgomeryshire adjacent to the border; see editor's note.

[4]Exx: GDG nos. 54, 84, 85, 88, 101, 137.

of Cynddelw and Hywel ab Owain Gwynedd[1] that due payment is expected for praise-poetry addressed to women, no less than from men. It may also be observed that Hywel ab Owain Gwynedd provides another kind of precedent for Dafydd, since he appears to complain of his failure[2] as often as to exult in his success in his love-affairs. These *rhieingerddi* of the Gogynfeirdd were addressed sometimes to girls, sometimes to married women[3] in the manner of the Provençal troubadours, and Dafydd ap Gwilym also has both kinds. It has been remarked[4] that his delineation of Dyddgu comes close to the outlines set in the earlier bardic tradition: the unmarried girls of the *rhieingerddi*, who possess, in addition to beauty of form and feature, the stock qualities of gentleness, courtesy, kindness and unaffected demeanour—qualities which are named in the bardic grammars[5] as the standard virtues for which nobly-born girls should be praised.

These are some of the ways in which the idiom and concepts of the older praise-poetry were carried over into the new medium. The metrical aspects of this transition have been the subject of particular examination by Dr. Parry, and I omit all reference to them here. Yet, ever since the content of Dafydd ap Gwilym's poetry has been the subject of comparative study, themes have been discovered in it which seem to correspond with elements in a very different poetic tradition—the conventions of *amour courtois* which originated in Provence in the eleventh century, and which were afterwards developed further in

[1]See *Oxford Book*, nos. 22 and 28. Similarly Gruffudd ap Dafydd ap Tudur records the gift of *aur a main* in payment for his poem to a girl, MA, 318 a; T. Gwynn Jones, *Rhieingerddi*, p. 32.

[2]Cf. T. Gwynn Jones, *Rhieingerddi*, pp. 13-14.

[3]The women named in Hywel ab Owain's *gorhoffedd* (*Oxford Book*, no. 22) are described as *gwragedd*: compare his two poems to girls (*ibid.*, nos. 23 and 24), and Cynddelw's *rhieingerdd* (*ibid.*, no. 28).

[4]T. Parry, 'Dafydd ap Gwilym', *Yorkshire Celtic Studies*, V. p. 26.

[5]G. J. Williams and E. J. Jones, *Gramadegau'r Penceirddiaid*, pp. 16, 35, 56; Saunders Lewis, *Braslun*, p. 87. Cf. GDG nos. 56; 79.

France, from whence they spread to England and to the other countries of Europe. The ultimate source for many elements in this poetic convention were the poems of Ovid—for the idea of Love as an art or science, which could be taught by precepts, and practised according to rules, for love as a sickness, and as a form of warfare. The Troubadours gave further development to these ideas: they exalted Love as an idealized form of service (there may have been here an implicit comparison with the feudal relation which bound a man to his lord), and a service which enjoined secrecy on its followers, so that they referred to their ladies under fictitious names. Even when unreciprocated, love must constitute its own reward. They developed the idea of Love's warfare by frequent references to the spears and arrows with which it was waged. It was the references to these things in Dafydd's *cywyddau* which Gruffudd Gryg regarded as artificial and alien to the whole tradition of Welsh poetry, as indeed they were. It was not that Dafydd exaggerated the perfections of Morfudd, for idealism of this kind would have been a recognized and accepted feature of bardic technique, but rather that he exaggerated their effect upon himself: what Gruffudd jeered at were the repeated references to the spears and arrows of love and to their disastrous effect upon Dafydd, bringing him near to death.[1] The charge made against him can indeed be substantiated from Dafydd's *cywyddau*, with their frequent allusions to the spears and arrows[2] and to the sickness and sleeplessness[3]

[1] For an important discussion of the significance of the *Ymryson* in Dafydd's poetry, see now Eurys Rowlands, *Y Traethodydd* CXXII (Ionawr, 1967), pp. 15-35 especially pp. 26-27. See also Glanmor Williams, *op. cit.* p. 192.

[2] *Gwayw, gwewyr* occur far more frequently in Dafydd's poetry than *saeth(au)*, but the figurative usage of these words seems to be in every respect equivalent, except that the first may have the secondary meaning of 'pangs', Exx: GDG 56, 11-14; 78, 45-46; 84, 17; 88, 13-14; 95, 43; 100; 111. Cf. Ifor Williams, *Trans.*, 1913-14, p. 160.;

[3] Exx: GDG 36, 17-28; 45, 15; 46, 43; 56, 4; 63, 1; 84, 5; 94 108. Note also the emphasis which is placed on secrecy, and the many

Continued on next page

caused by love, while the accompanying criticism of monotonously harping on a single theme is also admitted by Dafydd in the *cywydd* (GDG. 34) in which he says that, like the cuckoo, he has only a single tune to sing, and this is the theme of Morfudd's praise: *Unllais wyf . . . | â'r gog, morwyn gyflog Mai* (GDG. 34, 31-2). But it is worth remembering that Gruffudd's attack may well have derived additional force from the evidence of poems which have not survived. And the particular type of exaggeration of which he accuses Dafydd is to be found neither in Gruffudd Gryg's own *cywyddau* to girls nor in the few which have come down of the work of Dafydd's closer contemporaries, Madog Benfras and Iolo Goch. It is, however, a charge which any poet who took it upon himself to represent the accepted standards of the Welsh poetic tradition would feel justified in bringing against one who made use in his verse of the exotic elements in the continental convention of Courtly Love—elements which are only slightly and sporadically discernible in the work of any Welsh poet before Dafydd ap Gwilym.[1] It makes no difference to this charge of insincerity in his work that Dafydd's use of the foreign convention appears to be ironical more often than serious: he is accused of a type of innovation which led to a departure from the standards of truthfulness recognized in praise-poetry. Whereas the *cywyddau* to girls by Dafydd's contemporaries are a recognizable development from the earlier *rhieingerddi* of Hywel ab Owain Gwynedd and the other Gogynfeirdd

Continued from previous page

references to the necessity for it: GDG 30, 20; 40, 31-2; 74; 78; 98, 41 ff. These should not be overlooked in relation to the problem as to whether Dafydd is or is not using pseudonyms for the girls he addresses.

[1]The most significant of Dafydd's predecessors as regards his subject-matter is Gruffudd ap Dafydd ap Tudur (*circa* 1300; MA[2], pp. 318-20), and it is interesting that Dafydd actually repeats a couplet of his work (GDG 13, 23-24; see note). See T. Parry, *Hanes Llenyddiaeth Gymraeg*, p. 49; T. Gwynn Jones, *Rhieingerddi*, pp. 31-40; *Aberystwyth Studies*, IV, pp. 85-96.

poets, the continental attitude of extreme abasement in love which Dafydd chooses to affect at times is essentially alien to the *rhieingerdd*, and it is one which Gruffudd Gryg evidently considered that he demeaned his bardic status by adopting. In his reply to this onslaught, Dafydd does not, in fact, deny the substance of the accusation, for in calling his love-poetry *geuwawd o gywydd*, 'a *cywydd* of false praise' (GDG. 148, 6), he virtually admits that it is not defensible by the older standards of the bards. Nevertheless, he asserts that such a *cywydd* is, in a different way, as honourable as a praise-poem, for the things which some people have no use for can still be of value to others—and he backs up this claim with his striking metaphors of the rejected worn-out harp and the parchment scroll[1] or book which has become brown-edged and illegible: a use can be found for both of these in different strata of society from those which responded to aristocratic praise-poetry. And he counter-attacks by accusing Gruffudd of continuing to uphold an obsolete and exhausted tradition, because of the poverty of his own inspiration, and of carping criticism of the work of others—Gruffudd, he says, is *craig lefair beirdd*, the 'sounding-stone' or echo of the poets. The debate is continued throughout eight *cywyddau* which become increasingly abusive, as both poets resort increasingly to the traditional bardic armoury of satire. At the end, neither can be said to have won, and neither has fully answered the charge brought by his opponent. This lack of any final decision has been noted as a feature characteristic of medieval debates,[2] so that it is quite probable that the concluding *cywyddau* represents the end of the series, yet there is some evidence that there may have been a number of additional poems in the *Ymryson* which have not survived.[3]

[1]On *cwrrach*, see J. Lloyd-Jones, *Ériu*, XVI, p. 125.

[2]See J. W. H. Atkins, *The Owl and the Nightingale* (1922), p. lviii.

[3]A note in *Llanstephan MS.*, 133 reproduced by J. H. Davies, *Trans.*, 1905-6, p. 72, reports a tradition that there were twenty-two

Continued on next page

The charge which Gruffudd brings against Dafydd,
virtually that of undermining the tradition by introducing
into Welsh poetry alien concepts and conceits, is, therefore, corroborated by Dafydd's own *cywyddau* in such a
way as to distinguish them from the poems addressed to
girls by his contemporaries. Since the origin of these
conceits is clearly traceable among the stock conventions
of the continental code of Courtly Love, I shall limit my
discussion of foreign influences in this paper to a consideration of the sources from which Dafydd could have
derived these elements in his poetry. In the course of
trying to discover these, it has seemed to me that Dafydd's
rejections, if we could know more about them, might
prove almost as significant as what he chose to accept from
foreign models, and that characteristics which throw light
on his individual genius are, perhaps, to be traced in the
very nature of his response to such external influences as
reached him. But in commenting on this response, I shall,
of course, only be tackling a small part of the subject of
innovation in the style and matter of Dafydd's poetry.

First of all, then, the references which Dafydd makes to
Ovid, who is the single literary authority to whom he ever
refers by name. Many of the basic conceits of Courtly Love
are ultimately derived from Ovid's poetry, and he is
constantly cited by the poets of this convention (as, for
instance, by Chrétien de Troyes) and, indeed, by medieval
writers in general, as the paramount authority on all
matters relating to love. For Dafydd, *llyfr Ofydd*, 'the book
of Ovid', has practically come to mean 'the affairs of love',
and he refers to himself as *dyn Ofydd*, 'Ovid's man', and to
love-songs as *ofyddiaeth*. Evidence for the actual knowledge
of Ovid's work in Wales goes back to much earlier times,
and to the oldest sources of written Welsh, for among the
ninth-century glosses in Bodleian MS. *Auctor. F.4.32*—

cywyddau in the *Ymryson*. The substance of this passage is quoted in
the introduction to the 1789 *Barddoniaeth Dafydd ap Gwilym*, pp. xviii-
xix and *n*.

Zeuss's *Oxoniensis Prior*—are Welsh glosses on the first book of the *Ars Amatoria*.[1]   One or two possible references to Ovid occur in Welsh poetry before the time of Dafydd, including one in a love-poem by Hywel ab Owain Gwynedd, but all apparent references now need to be carefully scrutinized in the light of the late Professor J. Lloyd-Jones's study of a number of bardic compounds which contain the second element *ofydd*, and which he has shown may arise from a modified or a lenited form of one or other of two separate words, *dofydd* and *gofydd*, meaning 'ruler', 'afflictor' or the like.[2]

Dafydd ap Gwilym's poetry, then, provides the earliest incontrovertible allusions to the poet Ovid in Welsh, and the chief point of interest raised by these allusions is, of course, the question of whether or not Dafydd can have had any direct knowledge of the poet's work at all, or whether his citations merely reflect hearsay knowledge of Ovid's reputation, combined with the medieval fondness for an appeal to authority. The question is complicated by the fact that so many of the stock Ovidian ideas—Love as a form of warfare, as an art, and as a sickness—as well as the Ovidian characters of the old hag, the churlish doorkeeper, and the possessive 'husband'—became taken up into the courtly and bourgeois traditions[3] in French poetry at an early stage, and could have reached Dafydd by any one of a number of indirect channels, among others, the *Roman de la Rose*. The *Ars Amatoria* was the first of Ovid's works to become widely known in the vernacular:[4] more than one translation into Old French was made in the course of the

---

[1]Zeuss, *Grammatica Celtica*, 1054-1059; BBCS V, pp. 1-8; VI, pp., 112-5.

[2]BBCS XV, pp. 198-200.

[3]That is, into both romance and *fabliau*. See C. Muscatine, *Chaucer and the French Tradition* (California, 1960), chapters II and III.

[4]For French versions of Ovid, see Gaston Paris, *La Poésie du Moyen Age* (Paris, 1885), pp. 192-208; *Histoire Littéraire de la France*, vol. XXIX, pp. 455-525.

twelfth and thirteenth centuries, and it has, at various times, been suggested[1] that Dafydd could have known the *Ars Amatoria* through the medium of one of these. It is interesting, therefore, to find that in the earliest extant French translation of this work, Ovid is brought up to date for twelfth-century France by making the church take the place of the Roman theatre, and clerical mystery plays that of the race-course, as suitable meeting-places at which to encounter girls[2]—although, of course, it is hardly necessary to suggest any authority other than actual custom for the various passages in which Dafydd ap Gwilym refers to such meetings in church, as in the two well-known poems in which he alludes to the suitability of Llanbadarn church and Bangor cathedral for this purpose (GDG. nos. 48, 111).

This point of contact with the French adaptations of the *Ars Amatoria* may, therefore, be entirely fortuitous, and if we discount it, I can see no incontrovertible evidence in Dafydd's work for any direct knowledge of the *Ars Amatoria*. But there is another work of Ovid which offers a series of far more striking resemblances to poems by Dafydd. In the *cywydd* (GDG. 71) in which he apostrophizes the river Dyfi in spate, he beseeches it not to prevent him from crossing to Llanbadarn to visit Morfudd. In Ovid's work, the *Amores*[3] there is an address to one of the Italian rivers, swollen with melted snow, which prevents the poet, in a similar way, from crossing to visit his lady. Each poet, in apostrophizing the river, claims that it ought to sympathize with him as a lover: Ovid points out

---

[1] W. Lewis Jones, *Trans.*, 1907-8; W. J. Gruffydd, *Trans. of the Guild of Graduates*, 1908, p. 32.

[2] Kuhne and Stengel, *Maistre Elie'e Ueberarbeitung der ältesten franz. Uebertragung von Ovid's Ars Amatoria* (Marburg, 1886), pp. 37 ff. Cf. G. Paris, *La Poésie du Moyen Age*, pp. 192-3; L. P. Wilkinson, *Ovid Recalled*, p. 387.

[3] *Amores*, III, 6. Mr. Gerald Morgan drew my attention to this remarkable parallel some while before I had started on this investigation.

that rivers too have been in love, and gives a long list of the loves of various rivers for nymphs, while Dafydd claims that no one has praised the wave of the Dyfi so much, or compared it to so many different things—its strength to the shoulder of a horse or man, its voice to a harp or an organ, and so on. I am not aware that any close parallel, other than Ovid, can be found for Dafydd's *cywydd*, and I think that this by itself offers at any rate a presumption that Dafydd knew of the *Amores* in some form. In addition, it gives significance to other passages in the *Amores*, not paralleled elsewhere in Ovid, which are highly suggestive in comparison with certain of Dafydd's poems. These are the symbolic dream,[1] for which Ovid seeks an interpreter, in which his lady is personified as a white heifer; the discussion as to whether a soldier or a poet makes a more desirable lover;[2] and the figure of the slave who acts as a churlish doorkeeper,[3] keeping the girl shut away behind a creaking door. Each of these incidents has its separate parallel in one or other of Dafydd's *cywyddau*, and, taken as a group, they do seem to be highly suggestive. However, I shall presently point out that there exist other parallels which are much closer in treatment to Dafydd's rendering of these themes, in certain Old French poems which have come down. The Ovidian parallel to the address to the river Dyfi is the only one of these themes of which I do not know of any other vernacular version, but, of course, this does not mean that none such existed in the past. What the evidence seems to amount to, then, is merely this, that if Dafydd ap Gwilym had any knowledge *at all* of Ovid's poetry in the original, it is more likely to have been of the *Amores* than of any other of his works. This is the more interesting because the *Amores*, unlike the *Ars Amatoria*, was, apparently, among the less well-known of Ovid's works in the Middle Ages, for no early vernacu-

[1] *Amores*, III, 5.
[2] *Amores*, III, 8.
[3] *Amores*, I, 6; II, 12.

lar translations of it appear to have come down.[1] He
gives no indication anywhere of having had any knowledge
of Ovid's *Metamorphoses*, and this, generally speaking, was
the most widely quoted and influential of all Ovid's works
in the fourteenth century; but then, Dafydd had his own
inheritance of native mythology and legend on which to
draw for those purposes of illustration and comparison for
which the poets of other nations made an extensive use of
the *Metamorphoses*.

The most important of the original works through which
Ovid's legacy was transmitted to the later Middle Ages
was, undoubtedly, the thirteenth-century French poem
known as the *Roman de la Rose*.[2] This is an immensely
long allegorical love-story, set within the framework of a
dream, and it formed the pattern for many later medieval
poems. The first part was composed about 1230 by
Guillaume de Lorris, but this poet died before completing
his work. Much of Ovid's teaching on the art of love is
unfolded in Guillaume's presentation of his various
allegorical and type-figures—Idleness, Fair Welcome and
Danger, and his conventional characters of the Friend, the
Slanderer, and the ancient hag who has charge of the girl.
But he left his long and involved narrative unfinished, to
be taken up some forty years later by a very different poet,
one Jean de Meun, whose continuation of the poem could
hardly present a greater antithesis. Just as the work of
Guillaume de Lorris is essentially courtly, idealistic and
youthful, and written from an aristocratic standpoint, so
Jean de Meun is cynical, middle-aged and expressive of
middle-class opinion. He was, however, a widely-read and
well-informed man, who used the framework of his
predecessor's unfinished poem as a means of popularizing
for a lay-audience his teaching and opinions on a great

[1] Cf. G. Paris, *Histoire Littéraire*, p. 488.
[2] ed. E. Langlois, *Société des Anciens Textes Françaises* (Paris, 1914-
1924). For more recent studies, see p. 8 *n* 1 above, also C. Muscatine, *op. cit.*, chs. II and III.

diversity of subjects, such as the hypocrisy of the mendicant orders, the faithlessness and unreliability of women (and he gives a poignant account of the trials of the Jealous Husband), together with his views on the nature of man and the universe: his opinions about almost everything, in fact, except for his predecessor's exposition of the doctrine of Courtly Love.

When we come to consider the evidence for Dafydd ap Gwilym's knowledge of this poem, it is worth remembering first that actual documentary evidence has come down for the existence of a manuscript of the *Roman de la Rose* in Glamorgan, and in the early years of the fourteenth century. Its significance has been noticed both by Chotzen and by Professor G. J. Williams.[1] The work is listed by name, together with three un-named manuscripts written in Welsh, among the confiscated possessions of a certain Llywelyn Bren (the steward of Gilbert de Clare), who was executed in 1317. This chance reference, so fortuitously preserved, is curiously suggestive in relation to Dafydd's literary background, both as regards time and also place. For scattered through Dafydd's work are a number of things for which the most likely source seems to be the poem by Guillaume de Lorris. Some of these, indeed, are among the commonplaces of Courtly Love: the spears and arrows, the sleeplessness, and the obligation of secrecy. The old woman who is, for Dafydd, one of the *Tri Phorthor Eiddig* (GDG. 80), could well have been suggested to him by the similar figure who appears in the *Roman de la Rose*. There is also the association of May with youth and love and generosity, together with the opposite view, that the old and miserly must have an antipathy to the spring-time, and an affinity only with winter. The custom which Dafydd refers to so frequently, of bestowing the *cae bedw* or garland of birch-twigs by one lover on another, whatever be its origin, certainly suggests the

[1]Chotzen, *op. cit.*, p. 110; G. J. Williams, *Traddodiad Llenyddol Morgannwg*, p. 146.

French custom of bestowing garlands of flowers and leaves,
which appears in the *Roman* and is, indeed, a common-
place in Old French poetry, being apparently connected
with May-Day observances.[1]   There are a number of
other suggestions in Dafydd's work pointing to influences
from the *Roman de la Rose*: it could have been from the
Roman that Dafydd derived the idea for the allegorical
presentation of his breast as a fortress given to him to
defend (GDG. 140), while his simile of the Bird-Catcher
(GDG. 30), in which he presents himself as caught by a
girl's eyes like a bird trapped in bird-lime beside a pool,
has a striking parallel in the image of the fountain of
Narcissus, also representing the girl's eyes, by which the
lover is entrapped at the beginning of the *Roman*.[2] Taken
by themselves, perhaps none of these resemblances would
appear conclusive, but Dafydd has one image which is so
closely paralleled in the work of Guillaume de Lorris that
I find it impressive as evidence for his actual knowledge of
the French poem. This is the husbandry simile,[3] of the
lover who has sown his grain and watched it grow, only to
find it destroyed by a storm just before it is harvested.
Guillaume's lover applies this rather unusual simile to
himself at the point when the girl has been taken away
from him and shut up so that he cannot reach her. Dafydd
elaborates the same image throughout a whole poem
(GDG. 87), and with a wealth of technical terminology:
he has nourished his love like winter-tilth, it has been
ploughed and harrowed, and in the early summer en-
closed against the time of reaping, but suddenly the wind
changed (presumably with Morfudd's marriage) and the
poet's tempestuous tears caused the crop to be lost. This
poem seems to me to be as persuasive evidence for

---

[1]See G. L. Marsh, 'Chaplets of Leaves and Flowers', *Modern Philology*, IV (1906-7), pp. 153 ff; D. A. Pearsall (ed.) *The Floure and the Leafe* (Nelson, 1962), pp. 27-8.

[2]Cf. C. S. Lewis, *Allegory of Love*, pp. 128-9. *Roman*, ll. 1537-1614.

[3]*Roman*, ll. 3960-70. Cf. Chotzen, *op. cit.*, pp. 331-2.

Dafydd's direct knowledge of the work of Guillaume de Lorris as is his poem to the Dyfi for his knowledge of Ovid's *Amores*.

The *Roman de la Rose* was not an isolated work. It was, rather, the culminating expression of a whole trend or tradition in thirteenth-century French poetry, from which it sprang, and which continued to exist alongside it. In examining other works which belong to this tradition,[1] I came upon a number of features which seem to me to be relevant to the consideration of French influences upon Dafydd ap Gwilym, although these features have not been retained in the *Roman* itself. From about 1200, a type of dream-vision was popular in French and Anglo-Norman literature, which had a framework consisting in a forest or garden scene on a May morning, in which a paean of bird-song heralds the appearance of the god or goddess of Love, who comes to arbitrate between disputants upon a question of love, which either may or may not be personal to them in its application. In some of the earliest of these poems, it is the birds themselves who represent the jury, so to speak, since it is they who debate the problem at issue. And one of the most popular subjects of this bird-debate is the question as to whether, in human society, the clerk or the knight is the most desirable lover for a woman—or as a variant, whether any but clerks and knights are in fact entitled to love at all. It has been pointed out above that this theme occurs already in Ovid's *Amores*,[2] and it has certain medieval Latin intermediaries before it re-appears in French and Anglo-Norman, set within the framework of

---

[1] I am here above all indebted to E. Langlois, *Origines et Sources du Roman de la Rose* (Paris, 1891), and to C. Oulmont, *Les Débats du Clerc et du Chevalier* (Paris 1911). See also E. Faral, 'Les Débats du Clerc et du Chevalier' in his *Sources Latines des Contes et Romans Courtois du Moyen Age* (Paris, 1913); W. A. Neilson, *The Origins and Sources of the Court of Love* (*Studies and Notes in Philology*, VI, Harvard, 1899).

[2] *Amores*, III, 8.

the bird-debate.[1] In every version that has come down, with a single exception,[2] judgement is given consistently in favour of the clerk against the knight—an indication, of course, as to the presumed authorship of the poems. Another theme of the dream-visions, also attested previously in the *Amores*, is the pursuit and capture of a magic animal,[3] who is interpreted as representing the girl sought after by the dreaming poet. In one poem,[4] the judgement given by Venus on a question of love is preceded by a service of the Mass at which all the birds assist in their different capacities. Again, a sequel to some of the bird-debates consists in the death of the lover whose cause has lost, and his or her burial within the precincts of the garden of Love, in a tomb surrounded by birds who sing incessantly for the lover's soul.[5]

These four themes present striking parallels with certain of the *cywyddau*. Dafydd ap Gwilym gives a personal application to his discussion of the comparative merits of the clerk and the knight, for he puts forth the clerk's point-of-view in his own person (GDG. 58). He adduces arguments in his own favour, and against the merits of

---

[1]The relevant poems are *Concilium Romarici Montis, Altercatio Phyllidis et Florae*; *Blanchfleur et Florence*; *Florence et Blanchfleur*; *Melior et Idoine*; *Li Fablel dou Dieu d'Amors*; *De Venus la Déesse d'Amor*. On the Latin poems, see Raby, *Secular Latin Poetry* (Oxford, 1934), II, pp. 290-296.

[2]The Anglo-Norman *Blanchefleur et Florence* (Oulmont, *op. cit.*, p. 40).

[3]*La Panthère d'Amors* by Nicole de Margival, *circa* 1300 (ed. H. Todd, SATF Paris, 1883); cf. *Amores*, III, 5. See *n.* 73 below.

[4]*La Messe des Oiseaux* by Jean de Condé (ed. A. Scheler, *Dits et Contes de Baudouin de Condé et de son fils Jehan de Condé*, Brussels, 1866-7), Vol. III, pp. 1 ff.

[5]*Blanchefleur et Florence*; *Li Fablel dou Dieu d'Amors*; *De Venus la Déesse d'Amors*. Mr. Peter Dronke has suggested to me that in the poems of bird-mass and bird-requiem we have yet another theme which is ultimately derived from Ovid's *Amores* (II, 6), and from Statius' *Silvae* (II, 4).

the soldier, which are closely similar to those employed in the French poems; and significantly enough, the version which comes nearest to Dafydd's treatment of the theme is one of the Anglo-Norman versions written in England.[1] Dafydd has two poems recounting dream-experiences: one is his poem about the clock at Aberhonddu (GDG. 66), with its echo of earlier Celtic dream-belief, such as we meet in *Breuddwyd Maxen*, to the effect that the spirit actually leaves the body while dreaming. The other (GDG. 39) is the poem in which Dafydd dreams at day-break that he is in a forest, that he releases his hounds after a white doe, and that after a long pursuit she turns and comes to him for protection. This allegorical dream is interpreted for him by an old woman: the white doe represents the girl he is seeking, and the hounds are his *llateion* or love-messengers. This type of enigmatic or symbolic dream, which could only be understood by means of a skilled interpreter, belonged to one of the recognized medieval divisions of the *somnium*, according to the popular commentary on dreams by Macrobius.[2] Both Dafydd's dream poems bear witness to the intense interest which was commonly felt in the Middle Ages in the significance and interpretation of dreams. As for the

[1] *Melior et Idoine*. Some parallels are quoted by Chotzen, *op. cit.*, p. 229.

[2] *Macrobius: Commentary on the Dream of Scipio*. Translated by W. H. Stahl (Columbia, 1952), Bk. I, ch. 3; see also W. C. Curry, *Chaucer and the Mediæval Sciences* (revised edition, 1960), pp. 199, 207-8. The *cywydd* GDG 39 is of great interest in several ways; firstly, because of what we may call the literary history of the White Doe in Celtic and Romance sources (on this see my paper 'Celtic Dynastic Themes and the Breton Lays', *Études Celtiques*, IX, pp. 117-152); and, secondly, because the setting given to it links Dafydd's poem with the special treatment given to this theme in the continental poems, in which the hunt for a heroine who is transformed into a doe or other animal is one of the various possible elements of which the dream-vision is composed, just as the bird-debate is another. For the dream-belief reflected in GDG 66, see *Llên Cymru*, II, 206; V, 119.

Bird-Mass, Chotzen has already drawn attention to the
resemblance between the early fourteenth-century poem
by Jean de Condé, *La Messe des Oiseaux*,[1] and Dafydd's
cywydd, Offeren y Llwyn, 'The Woodland Mass' (GDG. 122).
But he did not point out that the French poem is inset in
the typical dream-framework, that it takes place in a
woodland setting, and is presided over by Venus, the love-
goddess, and that it precedes a bird-debate on a question
of love. In the French poem, the nightingale officiates,
and definite parts of the service are assigned in every
detail to the blackbird, the lark, the thrush, the linnet, the
chaffinch, and others. The nightingale and the thrush are
the only birds specifically mentioned by Dafydd. There
is, however, a striking resemblance in the handling of the
theme of the Mass in the two poems; and in both, the
audacious parallel with divine service goes so far as to
include the elevation of the Host, which, for Dafydd, is a
leaf, for Jean de Condé, a red rose. Even so, I feel very
doubtful as to whether Jean de Condé's poem can properly
be regarded as a source for Dafydd's treatment of the same
theme. The case here for a direct source is very different
from that which I have advocated in respect to the two
cywyddau—Hwsmonaeth Cariad and *Y Don ar Afon Dyfi*—
since in each of these poems the imagery presents a
striking and virtually isolated[2] parallel with an external
source. On the other hand, the recurrence of imagery in
which birds and bird-song are described in terms of the
service of the Mass, and its ministers and accessories, is so
frequent in Dafydd's *cywyddau*, and indeed so fundamental
to his poetic thought, that the manner in which he
envisaged birds as poets and preachers can hardly be con-

---

[1]Cf. Chotzen, *op. cit.*, pp. 187-8, and note 4, p. 32 above.

[2]There is one other instance of the metaphor of sowing the seed of
love in Dafydd's work: *Heodd i'm bron . . . | had o gariad . . . | heiniar cur*
(GDG 102, 5-7). Metaphors concerned with sowing the seed of
praise-poetry also occur, but these are not exactly parallel (GDG 7,
36; 34, 16; 133, 38).

sidered as conscious imagery at all. To him, birds were natural poets in their own right, singing in the court of the woods as he did in human courts, and indeed, praising God in the service of their song. Moreover, the implicit parallel which was felt to exist between bird-song and church-services is expressed widely in medieval literature.[1] The significance of Jean de Condé's poem would be much less, I think, if it were not that the French poem belongs also to the complex of dream-visions and bird-debates. Nevertheless, it seems to me more likely that in this case the influence was contributory and indirect rather than literary and direct, for it sometimes happens that external models may give a vigorous stimulus to tendencies already manifest or latent in a national literature. This is a point to which I must return later in connexion with the *Ymddiddanion* between men and birds which are prominent in the *canu rhydd*.

Finally, the French bird-debates on the Clerk *versus* Knight controversy in at least three instances combine this theme with that of the burial of a victim of love, in a tomb surrounded by birds who sing in perpetual chorus about it. The *cywydd*[2] describing the poet's burial for love has been rejected by Dr. Parry from the canon of Dafydd's authentic work, but it is too important in this connexion to be omitted from the discussion on that account. In this poem, the poet says that if he dies for love he will be buried in the forest, the church will be one of summer leaves with an altar of branches, seagulls will carry his bier, a chorus of birds will sing the service and the cuckoo will chant paternosters and psalms. A curious point is that one[3] of the French poems which provides a parallel for this theme

---

[1] Cf. Chaucer's *Book of the Duchess*, ll. 301-305. Some of the numerous French examples are cited in the references to birds' 'Latin', p. 36, *n.* 1 below.

[2] *Oxford Book*, no. 61; DGG , pp. 28-30.

[3] *Li Fablel dou Dieu d'Amors* (ed. Oulmont, *op. cit.*), st. XXV: *Puis apiela cantant en son latin | Tous les oysiaus ki a lui sont aclin.*

describes the language in which the birds sing as *son Latin*—their Latin. This phrase for bird-song is found in the *Roman de la Rose* and elsewhere in Old French poetry, most frequently in the typical May-morning context.[1] The Welsh poem refers to the *lladin iaith*, in which the birds sing the poet's obsequies. I have so far failed to discover, or to hear of, any other occurrence of this expression for bird-song in Welsh poetry of the period: its occurrence here, even if the poem is not by Dafydd, seems unmistakably to corroborate the evidence for the underlying influence of the French poems of bird-debate.[2]

In view of the importance of these bird-debate poems among the foreign literary influences which seem to have reached Dafydd ap Gwilym, I think it is significant that of all the creatures who are individually delineated in his work, it is birds alone whom he endows with the power of speech—and indeed, with the ability to use this power on occasion somewhat caustically. The Cock-Thrush, certainly, gives the poet advice entirely to his own mind about the enjoyment of the birch-woods in May (GDG. 36), but the other two birds who address him adopt an aloof and even critical attitude. The Woodcock is the only one of the *llateion* or love-messengers commissioned by Dafydd who roundly refuses the embassy suggested to him, on the grounds that it is too late in the year and too cold for such a journey, and that because of his delay the girl has chosen another companion (GDG. 115). The Magpie, busily occupied with her mate in building their nest of leaves and mud, offers Dafydd the gratuitous advice that he would be better sitting at home by the fire than getting wet out in

---

[1]*Roman de la Rose*, I. 8408. For further references, see Tobler-Lommatzch, *Alt-französische Wörterbuch*, s.v. *latin*. In the parallel English examples there is confusion between *laeden* (<*Latinum*) and the native *leden, loeden,* 'language'; see NED, s.v. *leden*.

[2]The *lladin* of the Owls in R. Williams-Parry's lyric (*Cerddi'r Gaeaf*, p. 6) is but one of the many echoes of Dafydd ap Gwilym which occur in this poet's work.

the wood pining for love, and that in any case he had better give up his unrewarded suit and become a hermit (GDG. 63). The contrast here indicated between the Magpie's productive, nest-building activity and the fruitless unproductive love of the poet is paralleled in Old French lyrics of the type known as the *reverdie*[1]—poems of greeting to spring, which also sometimes make this contrast between the poet's thwarted love and the mating of birds. Dafydd's ironic use of the convention is apparent: *Cyngor y Biogen* is, in its way, as forcible an indictment of his affected subservience to the code of Courtly Love as is Gruffudd Gryg's attack, or that of the Grey Friar; only that here, Dafydd imagines the indictment as coming from the words and actions of a *bird*.

In portraying his admonitory birds in this way, Dafydd seems to be drawing on some kind of antecedent popular tradition; one would like to know whether this had already taken shape in earlier Welsh poetry which has since been lost. There are, of course, a number of precedents in Welsh, as elsewhere, for talking birds; whether prophetic, or didactic,[2] or endowed with the wisdom which comes

---

[1] Cf. G. L. Brook, *op. cit.* (p. 8, *n.* 1 above), p. 8 and no. 11; Theo Stemmler, *Die englischen Liebesgedichte des MS. Harley* 2253 (Bonn, 1962), pp. 129 ff. I am indebted to Mr. Peter Dronke for referring me to the following poems which represent early examples of the theme: *Levis exsurgit zephirus* in the eleventh-century 'Cambridge Songs' (*Oxford Book of Mediæval Latin Verse*, ed. Raby, 1959, p. 173, *Penguin Book of Latin Verse*, ed. F. Brittain p. 166); and William of Poitier's *Ab la dolchor del temps novel* (C. Appel, *Provenzalische Chrestomathie*, Leipzig, 1895, p. 51). Further instances, with some parallels from later Gaelic folk-poetry, are cited by Ó Tuama, *op. cit.* (p. 10, *n.* 2 above), pp. 108-9.

[2] The *Ymddiddan Arthur a'r Eryr* (BBCS II, pp. 272 ff) provides an earlier Welsh precedent, and one which, if we accept the editor's dating (*circa* 1150), must antedate the French bird-debates. So also must the englyn *Chwerdit mwyalch mewn celli* (*Gramadegau'r Penceirddiaid*, p. 9), which Dafydd ap Gwilym knew and quoted (GDG 76, 23-28), and which reflects the same popular attitude to birds as *exempla*. On the source of the *englyn*, cf. Chotzen, *op. cit.*, p. 86.

with great age, like the Eagle, the Owl and the Blackbird, who are classed among the Oldest Animals in *Culhwch ac Olwen*. The wisdom of birds is proverbial in folk-poetry. The rather numerous *areithiau* and *ymddiddanion* which have come down in the *canu rhydd*—dialogues between a bird and a man who has come to ask its advice[1]—are significant in this respect. Although they go back only to the sixteenth century in their extant form, the general and, at times, the close resemblance in points of detail which they present with certain of Dafydd's *cywyddau* cannot, I think, be entirely accounted for as due to the influence of the *cywyddau* upon them.[2]   There are, indeed, certain marked differences in treatment between the *cywyddau* and the free-metre poems, which indicate that direct influence of the one upon the other can only be superficial, and that two separate poetic traditions are here involved. There is nothing in the later Welsh poems at all like the elaborate *dyfalu* of the bird or animal addressed, or the directions for its journey, which characterize this class of Dafydd's *cywyddau*.[3]   One of the ultimate models for these dialogues in the *canu rhydd* must lie in the French bird-debate poems to which I have referred: if these were already established in Welsh popular poetry by the fourteenth century, then Dafydd ap Gwilym is as likely to have imbibed these influences through the popular poems which were the prototypes of those which have come down,[4] as he is to have derived them from a direct knowledge of the originals.

The differences between the *cywyddau* and the *canu rhydd* are indeed in themselves a measure of those very

[1]*Canu Rhydd Cynnar*, nos. 33-36, *et passim*; cf. also p. lxxxiii, *n.* 2. As with Dafydd ap Gwilym, these poems overlap with the *llatai* poems, but also exist independently of this theme.

[2]Brinley Rees, *op. cit.*, pp. 65-6; D. Gwenallt Jones, *Y Ficer Prichard a 'Canwyll Cymyry'*, p. 44.

[3]Brinley Rees, *op. cit.*, p. 69.

[4]For opinions and inferences as to the antiquity of the tradition underlying the sixteenth-century *canu rhydd*, see *CRCy*, pp. xvi, xx; and cf. Ifor Williams, *Trans.*, 1913-14, pp. 115-6.

qualities in which Dafydd's poetry strikes us as most remarkable when set against the background of medieval poetry in other languages: that is, in his inspired observation of wild life, and in the imaginative command of language which enabled him to impart some of his own heightened vision. In his expression of this sense of fellowship with wild nature, combined with wonder at nature's 'infinite variety', Dafydd ap Gwilym's poetry looks back in a significant manner to an earlier Celtic precedent: that is, to the early Irish hermit verse, which offers a similar vision of community with nature, and one which is expressed with a comparable clarity and directness.[1] Here, then, it seems to me that Dafydd, with his unique gifts, is but giving individual expression to an attitude towards nature which is itself deeply rooted in the Celtic tradition, and one which has found recurrent expression in its literature at different periods. But it is an attitude which implies as strong a contrast as possible between Dafydd's portrayal of bird-life and that which we find in the French poems and in the Welsh *canu rhydd*, whose bird-protagonists are, in both cases, only thinly-disguised human beings. Only in his presentation of the

---

[1]Apparently Alfred Nutt was the first person to observe this affinity; see his edn. of *Arnold's 'Celtic Literature'* (1910), Appendix, p. 138. On this aspect of the hermit poetry, cf. K. Jackson, *Early Celtic Nature Poetry*, pp. 108-9: '. . . The ultimate significance of the hermit's relationship with nature is some thing that transcends both nature and hermit alike. . . . Through it all, rarely expressed, always implicit, is the understanding that bird and hermit are joining together in an act of worship; to him the very existence of nature was a song of praise in which he himself took part by entering into harmony with nature.' The personification of the blackbird in one quatrain as a 'hermit who does not clang a bell' (K. Meyer, *Bruchstücke der älteren Lyrik Irlands* (Berlin, 1919), p. 66), deserves comparison with Dafydd ap Gwilym. For text and translation of this quatrain, see J. Carney (ed.), *Early Irish Poetry* (The Mercier Press, Cork, 1965), pp. 11-12. trans. K. Jackson, *op. cit.* p. 11, *no.* x.

nightingale as essentially the bird of love,[1] do we seem to
find in Dafydd's poetry any kind of echo of the characteristics attributed to birds in the French bird-debates. A
parallel to this rejection of the common medieval view-
point is seen in Dafydd's treatment of animals, as in the
cywydd (GDG. 22), in which he describes his sudden vision
of the Fox, sitting unaware and unconcerned outside his
lair. The emphasis at the same time on the animal's total
self-absorption and on the vivid spectacle he presents is as
far removed as possible from the wily Reynard of the
French beast-epic, of which it seems impossible that
Dafydd would not have known,[2] and in terms of which
his contemporary, Geoffrey Chaucer, delineated *his* Fox.
But the subjective exploitation of the natural world was as
alien to Dafydd as were the allegorical abstractions and
psychological analysis of the poets who composed the
dream-visions and the *Roman de la Rose*. For he appears to
have had no sympathy for, or interest in, the fundamental
ideas which inspired these works, so that he rejected both
the high idealism of Courtly Love and the contrasting
cynicism to which it gave rise, and which is forcibly expressed in the work of Jean de Meun. But we can see that
while rejecting the spirit which informed them, and the
greater part of their substance as well, the things in these
foreign sources which acted as touchstones for his imagina-
tion were, in fact, most characteristic: that is, he found in
them suggestions for imagery, out of which he developed
and extended images of his own.

---

[1]Cf. J. Glyn Davies, *Trans.*, 1912-13, pp. 114-5, ' Whatever nucleus
of fact there may have been, there can be no doubt that it was the
European convention that kept the nightingale so much to the fore in
Dafydd's love-poetry.'

[2]It seems to have been after Dafydd's life-time that the fables of
Odo of Cheriton were translated into Welsh, late in the fourteenth
century (Ifor Williams, *Chwedlau Odo*, Wrexham, 1926). The Welsh
version contains a tale (no. XVI) in which the fox outwits Chantecleer
in typical fashion. Cf. Chaucer's 'Nonnes Priestes Tale'.

Any discussion of the content and style of Dafydd ap Gwilym's poetry must indeed resolve itself in the end into a discussion of his imagery, since this really implies an examination of his whole use of language, and of all but the purely metrical aspects of his work. The most immediately arresting of these images are, perhaps, the extended ones, (in his day a new thing in Welsh poetry), in which a metaphor or a simile is elaborated throughout a whole poem. One need but refer to such poems as *Morfudd fel yr Haul* (GDG. 42) or *Serch fel Ysgyfarnog* (GDG. 46), in addition to those I have already mentioned, or to the metaphor of the man shooting at a nightingale, in terms of which he refers to the death of the poet Gruffudd ab Adda (GDG. 18). But there is also the imagery which is implicit in his use of vocabulary, and here one must take count on the one hand of his recurrent use of the traditional and archaic phraseology of bardic poetry, loaded with evocative associations of a literary kind; and on the other hand, of his contrasting use of a vocabulary apparently simple and direct, but which may, in fact, be highly evocative in a different way. Dr. Parry and Mr. Eurys Rowlands, each by analysing a single poem,[1] have illustrated some of the nuances in meaning which Dafydd achieves in this way, whether or not by conscious intention. Alternative meanings may be suggested, either because of ambiguity in the meaning of a word itself, or in its pronunciation, or because of the association of ideas which it sets in train. Individual characteristics in Dafydd's practice of the art of *dyfalu*, related as it is to riddle-poetry, but also closely bound up with the evolution of the *cywydd* metre,[2] also need full investigation. In this connexion, Dafydd's frequent use of personification has been pointed

---

[1] Thomas Parry (on *Cywydd y Gwynt*), *Lleufer*, XII (1956), pp. 119 ff. Eurys Rowlands, 'Cywydd Dafydd ap Gwilym i Fis Mai', *Llên Cymru*, V, pp. 1 ff.

[2] T. Parry, *Trans.*, 1939, pp. 216-217; *Hanes Llenyddiaeth*, p. 91; D. Myrddin Lloyd, *Llên Cymru*, I, p. 164, *n.* 16.

out. Nature is interpreted in human terms—the summer is
teg wdwart 'a fair woodward' (GDG. 27, 3), the holly *gwas
tabarwyrdd*, 'lad with the green tabard' (GDG. 29, 28), the
stag *hardd farwn hir*, 'a fair tall baron' (GDG. 116, 16), and
he refers more than once to the 'hair' of the birchtree in
summer, *gwallt ar ben hoyw fedwen haf* (GDG. 24, 14). Just as
birds are described as preachers and priests, so, conversely,
Dafydd compares his fellow-poets to birds in his *marwnadau*
for them, and just as the sea-gull is a nun, *lleian ym mrig
llanw môr* (GDG. 118, 10), so in another poem nuns are
seen as swallows, *gwenoliaid* (GDG. 113, 20). Very new
and modern images may be used to gain immediacy of
impact and surprise effects, as in the poem on Envy with
its series of metaphors drawn from the organized defence
of contemporary fortifications (GDG. 140).[1]   In all these
ways, Dafydd may be said to have flouted tradition by
giving his audience the stimulus of what was new and
unexpected, in place of what was customary and weighted
with the *aura* of literary associations. Yet, after all, the
technique by which forceful and vivid comparisons are
attained by startling new associations of ideas was only the
re-appearance in a new form of something which was
itself very old in Welsh poetry, for it is the 'studied contrast' which Sir Ifor Williams has pointed out as a feature
of the earliest poetry,[2] appearing again in a new setting.

Another aspect of Dafydd's fondness for gaining effects
by using known words in unexpected contexts is to be seen
in the particular ways in which he employs borrowed
words of Romance origin.   These borrowed words,
whether they are taken directly from French, or indirectly
through the medium of Middle English, consist, as is not
surprising, almost entirely of nouns, and for the most part
of nouns denoting concrete things.   They are words for
buildings and furnishings of all kinds (in terms of which he
describes his woodland retreat in the *deildy* or *castell celli*);

---

[1]Cf. T. Parry, *Yorkshire Celtic Studies*, V, p. 29.
[2]*Lectures on Early Welsh Poetry* (Dublin, 1944), p. 33.

different kinds of weapons, especially the cross-bow, *arblastr*, and its adjuncts; and words for various types of currency—*coron, fflwring, copr, mwnai*, and so forth. There is also a less concrete series of words dealing with the law and official administration—*ustus, seiler, fforffed, ceisbwl*,[1] *corodyn*.[2] And when these borrowed words are used, they are employed far more often than not in a figurative sense, in that they are used right out of their normal prosaic context, to give the shock and stimulus of the unexpected.

The leaves of May are florins on the tops of the branches, they are *iawn fwnai*, 'true currency' (GDG. 23, 11);[3] the stars are golden pieces of wrought metal, *goldyn o aur melyn mâl* (GDG. 67, 36); ears are *ceiniogau cof* 'the pennies of memory' (GDG. 26, 10); everyone is only a copper coin compared with Madog Benfras, *copr pawb wrthaw* (GDG. 19, 44). Gruffudd Gryg is taunted with the epithet *arblastr*—he is a cross-bow for the number of words he hurls, shooting at every mark (GDG. 154, 1). The mist is a parchment-roll, making a surface for the imprint of the rain—*rhol fawr a fu'n glawr i'r glaw* (GDG. 68, 15), and in an elaborate sustained metaphor the cock-thrush is in turn sheriff, justice and steward of the court, reading a legal summons, again from a parchment-roll (GDG. 123). The nightingale is indicted *(ditio)*—that is, legally charged and then banished from Coed Eutun (GDG. 25, 52), and love is confirmed with the seal of a kiss *(inseilio, GDG. 133, 45).

Some of these types of imagery are exemplified in the work of Dafydd's contemporaries. Thus Gruffudd ab Adda speaks of the 'hair' of the birchtree,[4] and personifies

---

[1]'Catchpoll'. *Ceis* in this word may, however, be ultimately of Welsh derivation: see J. Russell-Smith, *Medium Aevum*, XXII, pp. 104-110.

[2]Idris Foster, *Medium Aevum*, XXIII, p. 43, compares Ml. Lat. *corrodium*, etc., Ml. Eng. *corrody*, 'supplies, maintenance', etc. The legal connotations of the word are apparent from the instances cited in NED and the *Middle English Dictionary* (Michigan).

[3]See D. Stephen Jones, BBCS XIX, p. 31, on this reference.

[4]*Oxford Book*, no. 54, l. 1.

its bare trunk, used as a May-pole, as *traetures llwyn*, 'traitress of the woodland'. It is interesting to find that Gruffudd Gryg describes the moon as *nobl* and *fflwring*,[1] since Dafydd also uses for the moon both *fflwring* and the disparaging word *polart* (GDG. 70, 57)—meaning in this case that it is a base coin appearing in place of the sun, providing light where it is not desired, but no warmth—it is even capable of being reduced in size as though it were a clipped coin.

Nevertheless, it seems to me that there are here certain types of imagery as to which we should consider carefully whether they may not be personally characteristic of Dafydd ap Gwilym. Many years ago, Mr. Saunders Lewis advocated as a significant personal trait of this kind the frequency of imagery which transfers all the conventional attributes of the *llys* to Dafydd's court in the woods;[2] a calculated reversal in his poetry of the conventional values of the bards, which Dafydd has summed up in the single line *Gwell yw ystafell, os tyf*, 'A room is best if it grows' (GDG. 121, 8). This concept may indeed have originated with Dafydd ap Gwilym, to be elaborated further by other poets, since Dr. Parry has detected late features in two of the *cywyddau* which best support the argument.[3] But there are other images which should be considered. These include the poet's frequent figurative use of two of the classes of borrowed words to which I have alluded—of words for coins and currency, and of imagery based upon legal words and concepts connected with official administration. In respect to the first, it has been pointed out by Professor T. Jones Pierce,[4] that the use of coinage was spreading into Wales during the fourteenth

[1]*Oxford Book*, no. 56, ll. 3, 14.

[2]*Braslun*, pp. 82-84.

[3]'Adeiliais dŷ fry ar fron' (BDG LXXXVII) and *Y Llwyn Banadl* (BDG XLVII, *Oxford Book*, no. 63). See GDG, pp. clxxi ff., nos. 1 and 164.

[4]*Wales Through the Ages* (1959), I, p. 157. References to currency are to be found in the work of earlier poets, but these are literal and

Continued on next page

century replacing the older custom of barter and payment in services. The figurative use of words for specific coins is extremely rare, and indeed exceptional, in the poetry of the period outside Dafydd's own work: Gruffudd Gryg's use of coin-images for the moon could have been suggested to him by Dafydd's own poem, since on internal evidence his *cywydd* must have been composed at the very end of the fourteenth century,[1] later than the period which is generally assigned to Dafydd's life-span. The rejected *Cywydd y Sêr*[2] refers to the stars as *dimeiau*, 'halfpennies', and here also the poet describes the darkness as surrounding him as though he were in a jail—*ynghanol geol gaead*. There is disagreement as to the authorship of this poem, and it has been argued by more than one writer that it should be restored to the canon of Dafydd's authentic work.[3] I think these images in it may, perhaps, provide some supporting evidence for doing so. Dafydd uses the same metaphor of the jail in his poem *Dan y Bargod* (GDG. 89), when he is waiting under the dripping eaves: *Ni bu'n y Gaer yn Arfon | Geol waeth no'r heol hon*. And there can hardly be a more forceful instance of this rather ominous type of imagery drawn from the world of official administration than his description of the Wind as endowed with

Continued from previous page
not figurative. Eg. Gruffudd ap Dafydd ap Tudur: *deugein swllt nod o ysterlingod* (RBP. 1255, 8). The stock metaphor which describes a girl's hair as *aur mâl* is common at all periods, and is attested already in the *Gogynfeirdd* (see T. Gwynn Jones, *Rhieingerddi*, p. 29; IGE. p. 3, l. 21; cf. Chotzen, *op. cit.*, p. 209). But it is, probably, gold as a substance, rather than gold coinage, which is here intended.

[1] See p. 16, *n.* 4 above.

[2] *Oxford Book*, no. 64.

[3] S. Lewis, *Llên Cymru*, II, p. 201; D. J. Bowen, *ibid.*, VI, pp. 44-5; VII, pp. 193-205. Iolo Goch uses *geol* figuratively of a ship (IGE[2], p. 74, l. 29), and there are instances of this type of metaphor in the work of Dafydd's younger contemporaries; e.g. Llywelyn Goch describes the snow-covered landscape as *cuchiog gwaeth na swyddog sir* (DGG[2] LXXXV, 11). The comparative prominence of these images in Dafydd ap Gwilym's poetry remains striking.

freedom to move everywhere unrestricted: *Ni'th dditia neb, ni'th etail / Na llu rhugl, na llaw rhaglaw*, 'No one accuses you, neither hand of governor nor swift host restrains you' (GDG. 117, 14).

Another feature which may well turn out to be distinctive concerns the arrangement of some of Dafydd's more elaborate images: in a number of the *cywyddau* these occur in triple groups.[1] For instance, in aspiring after Dyddgu, the poet compares his temerity firstly to some small climbing creature, a marten, pole-cat or squirrel, who ascends from branch to branch, but on reaching the top of the tree does not find it so easy to come down again; next, to the audacity of sailors who venture on the sea with only a thin plank between them and the deep (he, like them, cannot easily turn back); and, finally, to the marksman who, after many random shots, finally scores a bull's eye: may not Dafydd also aim successfully and win the girl in the end with his poems of praise (GDG. 37)? In another *cywydd* (GDG. 131) he cites a very different set of images in alluding to his persistency in the pursuit of Morfudd—he is like the flexible branch of an apple-tree which bends easily and yet does not break; like a starved old cat, long accustomed to being kicked and knocked about, who, in spite of all ill-treatment, nevertheless survives; and, finally, like one who reaches his destination by walking while others run. His protest against girls putting on ornaments to go to the fair (GDG. 49) is elaborated by reference first to the sun, which can have no need of additional brightness; then to an old broken bow, which is not to be mended merely by gilding it externally; and lastly, to a lime-washed wall which serves its function as a wall as well as one which is painted with coats-of-arms. Again (GDG. 60) he compares his fruitless endeavours to please a heedless young girl to the efforts of those who try

[1]On the triad as a rhetorical device in Welsh and Irish literature, see my essay *Matthew Arnold and Celtic Literature: A Retrospect* (Oxford, 1965), p. 13.

to tame wild animals, and describes in turn a hare, a squirrel and a roebuck; in each case, in spite of their fostering, their wild natures will cause them to make off to the wilds at the first opportunity. More cynically, he compares his position in relation to Morfudd's husband to that of one of the two oxen in a yoke, to a ball which is tossed from one hand to the other, and to a rejected empty barrel (GDG. 93). Morfudd's beauty, polluted as a result of her marriage, is compared to a splendid varnished carving in negligent keeping, to a valuable English fur destroyed by peat-smoke, and to an oaken palisade warped by the salt water of the sea (GDG. 81).[1] A variant of this triple arrangement is found in the *Ymryson*, when Dafydd backs his argument in favour of the despised *cywydd* by his vivid illustrations of the worn-out harp and the discarded poetry-book; to be answered by a similar triple arrangement in Gruffudd's rejoinder, when he compares Dafydd's poetry with the two other short-lived wonders recently seen in Gwynedd—the hobby-horse at the fair, and the new organ in Bangor cathedral. And there are, of course, the poems in which certain of the traditional triads are cited for comparison with the subject of his praise: *Tair gwragedd â'u gwedd fal gwawn* (GDG. 51), in which the girl is added as a fourth to the triad of the three women who inherited the beauty of Eve,[2] and the *cywydd* (GDG. 84) in which Morfudd's powerful fascination is compared with the enchantment of the Three Famous Magicians.[3] In *Tri Phorthor Eiddig* (GDG. 80), the gatekeepers of the Jealous Husband are the hound, the

---

[1]The exact interpretation of the involved passage ll. 25-34 is uncertain. I take *llugorn* (l. 28) and *gwiw ei lliw* (l. 32) as stock epithets for the girl, which in each case run parallel to the preceding image; if this interpretation is correct, the three main metaphors stand out clearly.

[2] *Trioedd Ynys Prydein*, no. 50.

[3]For variants, see TYP, nos. 27, 28, Appendix IV, 4. It is significant to find that Dafydd's comparison of a girls' attraction with the magic of Math is anticipated in the third of the *englynion* quoted

Continued on next page

creaking door, and the sleepless old hag—a triad which is actually quoted in a slightly variant form in one of the early *canu rhydd*.[1]

This fondness for triple groupings brings us back again to the importance in Dafydd's literary inheritance of the store of oral learning on all levels; not only the tradition of the bards, but also the humbler and much-less-well documented tradition which has, in part, come down in the *canu rhydd*. It is now recognized that the new poets of the *cywydd* in the fourteenth century took over from the *clêr* the popular measure of the *traethodl*, developing it and giving it *cynghanedd*. The evidence of the *canu rhydd* indicates that the same class of poets continued to use this and others of the oldest Welsh metres in an unbroken succession which comes to light for the first time in sixteenth-century manuscripts. It seems unlikely that Dafydd and his contemporaries, in following certain of the poetic devices of the *clêr*, and taking from them one of their metres, should at the same time have wholly neglected the kinds of subject-matter treated of by these humbler poets. And thus it is that perhaps the greatest of all the problems concerning the manner in which foreign literary influences reached Dafydd ap Gwilym (and one to which we can hardly hope ever to know the full answer) is that of determining how far this subject-matter included themes of ultimate French origin, and to what extent these themes were already established in Welsh poetry in the fourteenth century. As an instance, I have suggested that the influence of the French bird-debates, which we find well-attested in the *canu rhydd* at a later date, could as well have reached Dafydd through populars channels as from specific French literary models. Again, a few of Dafydd's

---

Continued from previous page

as examples in all texts of the early version of the bardic grammar, GP, pp. 7, 26, 46; BBCS. II, p. 191.

[1] *Oxford Book*, no. 108. A similar popular provenance may be suggested for the triad quoted GDG 137, 41-2: *Tri pheth a gerir drwy'r byd / Gwraig a hinon ac iechyd.*

cywyddau show certain not-very-close affinities with some of the well-marked types of the medieval French lyric. I have suggested a parallel between *Cyngor y Biogen* and one of the recurrent themes of the *reverdie*; parallels have also been pointed out to the themes of the *pastourelle*; the *malmariée*, in which a young girl is married to an old husband; the *serenade*; and the *aube*, or dawn-parting of lovers[1]—and some at least of these types recur also in the *canu rhydd*.[2] I think, then, that it is important to make a clear distinction between influences on Dafydd's poetry from specific literary works whose circulation must at all times have been through written channels—and here I have advocated the supreme importance for Dafydd's literary background of two works in particular, Ovid's *Amores* and the *Roman de la Rose*—and those indeterminate influences which could have reached him orally through songs and poetry current in Latin, French, English, and even Welsh. All these tongues must have been the medium of popular entertainment in the Norman boroughs

---

[1]Direct influence seems extremely doubtful in all cases. The parallels are discussed by Ifor Williams, *Trans.*, 1913-14, pp. 118-121 = DGG², pp. xl-xli. He compares GDG 41 with the *pastourelle* (cf. Brinley Rees, *op. cit.*, pp. 49-50); GDG 89 with the *serenade*; GDG 129 with the *aube* (cf. W. Lewis Jones, *Trans.*, 1907-8, pp. 146-7). This last poem deserves comparison with *Cyngor y Biogen* in that it almost approaches a parody of the foreign model. The authenticity of the second *aube*, BDG XCVII, discussed by Chotzen, *op. cit.*, pp. 290-2, is now rejected; see GDG clxxxiii, no. 117. This poem and GDG 129 have been discussed again recently (with translation) by Prof. Melville Richards in *Eos: An Enquiry into the Theme of Lovers' Meetings and Partings at Dawn in Poetry*, ed. by A. H. Hatto (The Hague, 1965), pp. 568-574. Dr. Geraint Gruffydd has made the interesting suggestion that the form of Dafydd ap Gwilym's elegy on his uncle (GDG 13) has been influenced by that of the *serenade; Ysgrifau Beirniadol* I, ed. J. E. Caerwyn Williams (Gee, 1965), pp. 131-132.

[2]Brinley Rees, *op. cit.*, chs. II and III. The poem *Crys y Mab*, *Oxford Book* no. 102, is a clear example of a *pastourelle*. The *reverdie* theme recurs again in the *ymddiddanion* with birds, see p. 38, *n.* 1 above.

established in Wales in the wake of the Conquest. We know that Dafydd ap Gwilym had close contact with these, and Mr. Saunders Lewis, in a striking article,[1] has stressed the polygot character of the community in which he must have grown up.

When we speak of Innovation, then, in reference to Dafydd ap Gwilym's poetry, we tend to mean either changes which he himself initiated, or at least such as appear for the first time in the poets of his generation: we think of the major metrical innovation of the fourteenth century, the development of the *cywydd*; and as regards subject-matter, of the new themes which appeared then in Welsh poetry for the first time, the new attitudes to life and society, the response to literary influences from abroad. But it is important to recognize also that Innovation in this sense may include the appearance for the first time in Dafydd's *cywyddau* of themes imbibed from the sub-literary tradition of popular poetry: for although it may be common for aristocratic modes to travel downwards, the opposite process is also a recognized phenomenon, and there is a tendency for elements in the humbler, more spontaneous kinds of poetry to come upwards and re-vitalize the tradition. This last is what Professor W. J. Gruffydd once called 'the vital impetus in the ancient literatures of the Celtic peoples'.[2] It may well have been principally through the vitality of this impetus that the new literary influences from abroad came to be combined with many of the oldest elements in the Celtic literary tradition in the poetry of Dafydd ap Gwilym.

[1]*Blackfriars*, March 1953, pp. 131-6.

[2]W. J. Gruffydd, *Dafydd ap Gwilym* (Gwasg Prifysgol Cymru, 1935) p. 33.

ABBREVIATIONS

BDG. *Barddoniaeth Dafydd ap Gwilym* (o grynhoad Owen Jones a William Owen), London, 1789.

BBCS. *Bulletin of the Board of Celtic Studies.*

CRCy. *Canu Rhydd Cynnar.* Casglwyd a golygwyd gan T. H. Parry-Williams (Gwasg Prifysgol Cymru, 1932).

DGG². *Cywyddau Dafydd ap Gwilym a'i Gyfoeswyr.* Wedi eu golygu gan Ifor Williams a Thomas Roberts (Gwasg Prifysgol Cymru, 1935).

GDG. *Gwaith Dafydd ap Gwilym.* Golygwyd gan Thomas Parry (Gwasg Prifysgol Cymru, 1952).

GDG². ibid (*Ail Argraffiad*, 1963).

GP. *Gramadegau'r Penceirddiaid.* Golygwyd gan G. J. Williams ac E. J. Jones (Gwasg Prifysgol Cymru, 1934).

IGE². *Cywyddau Iolo Goch ac Eraill* (Argraffiad Newydd). Golygwyd gan Henry Lewis, Thomas Roberts ac Ifor Williams (Gwasg Prifysgol Cymru, 1937).

NED. The *New English Dictionary.*